Upper Yellowstone River
Mapping Project

July 2001

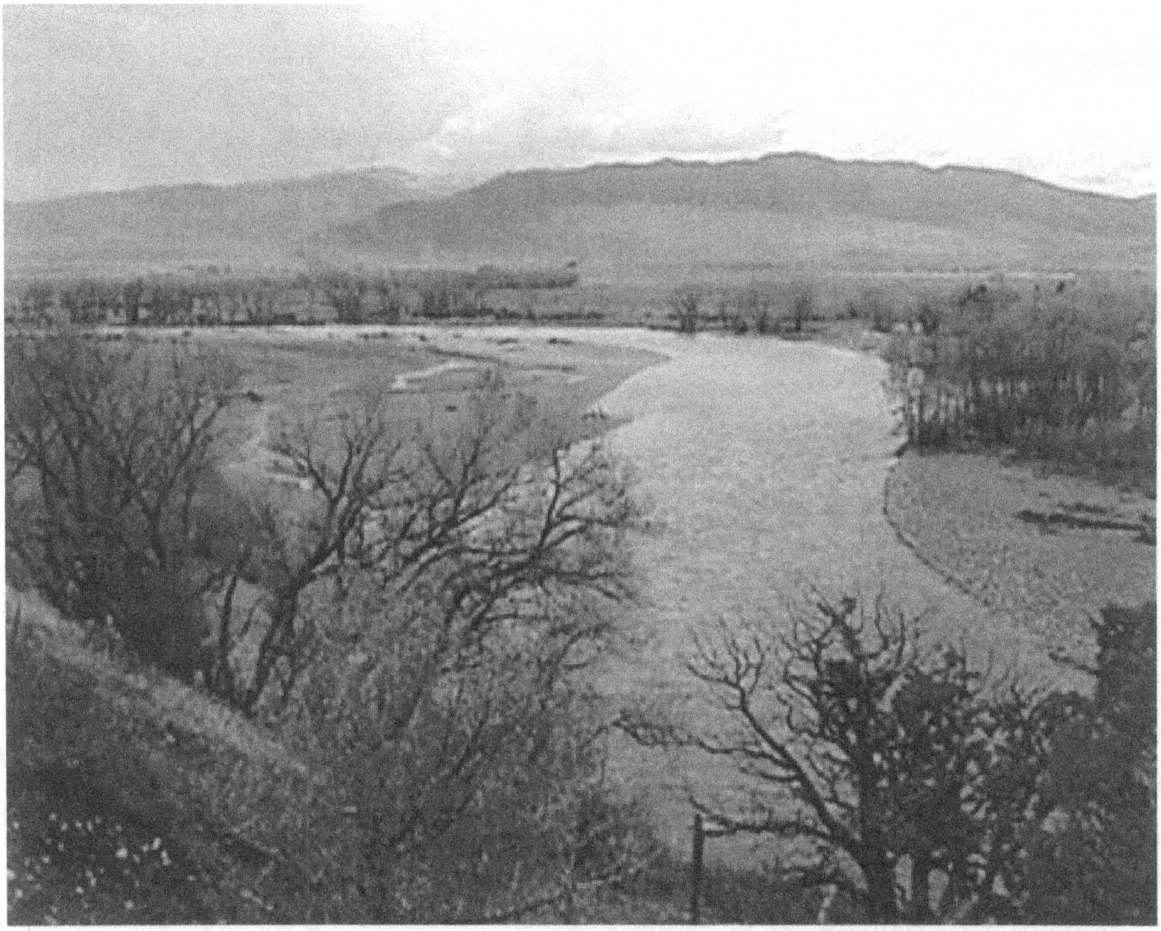

Kevin W. Bon
U.S. Fish and Wildlife Service
Denver, Colorado

Upper Yellowstone River Mapping Project

Contents

Introduction 1
Study Area 2
Mapping Procedures 4
    General 4
    Photography 4
    Field Work 4
    Photo Interpretation 5
    Cartography 6
    Digitization 8
    Quality Control 8
Mapping Conventions 9
    Wetland 9
    Riparian 10
    Upland 11
Products 13
Results 13
Definitions 18
Literature Cited 19
Appendix A: National Wetlands Inventory Map Legend used for the Yellowstone River . 20
Appendix B: Riparian Habitat Map Legend used for the Yellowstone River 21
Appendix C: Upland Land Use/Land Cover Classification Legend. 22
Appendix D: Wetland Classifications and Acreage Statistics 23
Appendix E: Riparian Classifications and Acreage Statistics 26
Appendix F: Upland Classifications and Acreage Statistics 28

List of Figures
    Figure 1. Project Area 3
    Figure 2. Example of Aerial Photography, and Color-coded Map 5
    Figure 3. Portion of NWI Map. 7
    Figure 4. Examples of Classification Terminology 12
    Figure 5. Riverine Classification Pie Diagram 14
    Figure 6. Palustrine Classification Pie Diagram 15
    Figure 7. Riparian Habitat Pie Diagram 16
    Figure 8. Upland Land Use/Land Cover Pie Diagram 17

Suggested Citation: Bon, K. W. 2001. Upper Yellowstone River Mapping Project. U. S. Fish and Wildlife Service. Denver, Colorado. 29 pp.

Cover photo: Yellowstone River in Paradise Valley.

Introduction

The Yellowstone River is the longest free-flowing river in the contiguous United States. It flows for six hundred seventy miles from it's headwaters in the Absaroka Mountains in northern Wyoming to it's juncture with the Missouri River in western North Dakota. Lewis and Clark descended much of the Yellowstone River during their Voyage of Discovery in 1806. The upper Yellowstone River within Park County, Montana is one of the west's premier native trout fisheries and supports populations of cutthroat trout. It also supports and regenerates stands of riparian cottonwood forest and provides habitat for neo-tropical migrant bird species. Flooding in 1996 and 1997 caused property damage with subsequent increases in channel modification activities. Given the resource significance of this area, issues have been raised regarding the effects of bank stabilization and long term cumulative impacts. Landowners and municipalities have attempted to prevent or reduce flooding and erosion through bank stabilization structures involving rock riprap and channel deflection using rock barbs. The Governor's Upper Yellowstone River Task Force was formed in November of 1997 to address the cumulative effects of existing and proposed channel modifications and to provide a cooperative forum for local comprehensive planning. Permitting agencies such as the U. S. Army Corps of Engineers, in cooperation with other Federal, state and local agencies, and private individuals require knowledge of this upper reach of the river to assist in deciding what effects these channel modifications will have on domestic, recreational and wildlife resources. A resource inventory of current habitat and land use along the river is the important first step in the development of comprehensive resource management plans and future decision making.

Debris deposited on a gravel bar during high flows on the Yellowstone River.

Bank stabilization using rip-rap along the Yellowstone River.

Study Area

The upper Yellowstone River was mapped from the northern boundary of Yellowstone National Park near Gardiner, Montana to the bridge which crosses the river at Springdale, Montana (Figure 1). This is a reach of approximately 84 river miles and is bounded laterally by specific elevation contours identified on USGS topographic maps. The mapped area of approximately 85 square miles encompasses the majority of the area that has been flooded by the river in the last 300 years and therefore includes all wetland and riparian habitat adjacent to the river as well as surrounding land use. The study area covers all of the Paradise Valley where the majority of channel modifications have taken place. Portions of 14 topographic quads are covered in the study area including: Gardiner, Electric Peak, Dome Mountain, Miner, Dailey Lake, Emigrant, Pray, Dexter Point, Chimney Rock, Brisbin, Livingston, Mission, Elton and Springdale.

Figure 1. Upper Yellowstone River project area.

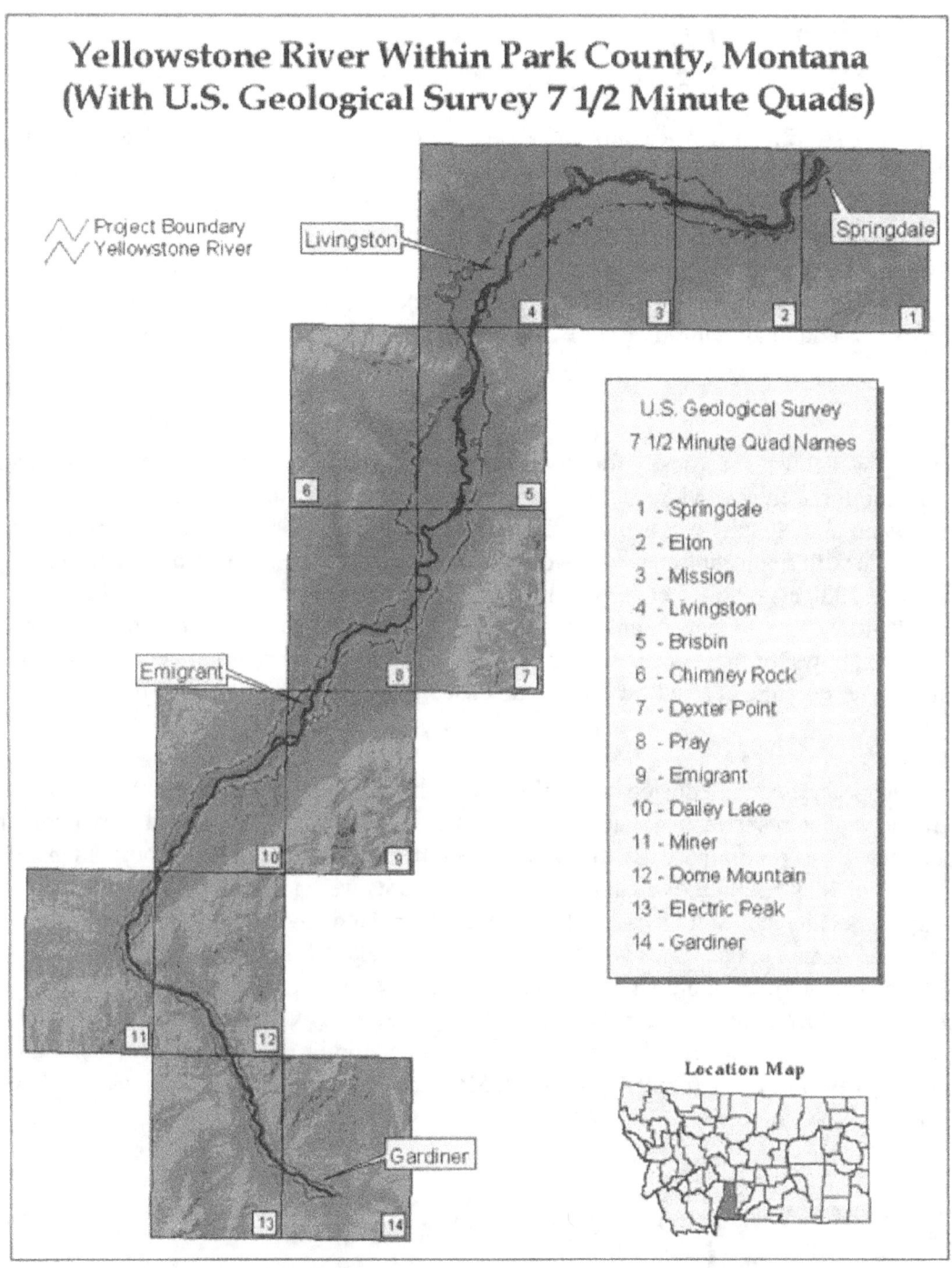

Mapping Procedures

General

Mapping of the study area was accomplished using remote sensing techniques. Remote sensing technologies provide the most accurate, cost effective and expeditious means for mapping large areas. Standard photo interpretation, cartography and digitization procedures were followed to produce final maps and digital data. All habitats (wetland and riparian) as well as land use and land cover were mapped. This mapping effort provides baseline spatial data for habitat and land use planning and management by identifying location and size of all habitats. Data exist as both hard copy maps and in digital format for ease of analysis using geographical information systems (GIS).

Photography

Photography was flown specifically for this project to provide the optimum scale, emulsion and time of season for accuracy in habitat discrimination. River flows were monitored prior to photo acquisition and photography was acquired on August 25 and 26, 1999 at a scale of 1:24,000 and is stereoscopic with a color infrared emulsion (Figure 2). Discharge at the time of photography was 3440 and 3330 cfs (cubic feet per second) respectively. This flow rate allowed more accurate identification of the main channel compared to river bars that are submerged during high flows. It also allows for more accurate differentiation of upland and riparian versus wetland since there is no flooding at low flow which can obscure the true habitat or land use.

Field Work

Field reconnaissance was conducted both prior to and during photo interpretation to correlate photographic signatures to distinct habitats and landscape features on the ground. Two field trips were conducted, one preliminary trip the week of October 5,1998 and another more intensive trip the week of May 7, 2000. Wetland and riparian habitats were identified in the field by hydrology, vegetation and soil types. Upland land use and land cover were identified by vegetation and human usage. Sites were checked on all quads within the study area to establish and confirm correlation of photo-signatures to specific cover types. U.S. Fish and Wildlife Service staff conducted field work in concert with the U. S. Army Corps of Engineers, Natural Resource Conservation Service, Montana Department of Natural Resources and Conservation, Montana Department of Environmental Quality, Montana Governors Upper Yellowstone River Task Force and the University of Montana.

Figure 2. Example of aerial photography and color-coded map of same area.

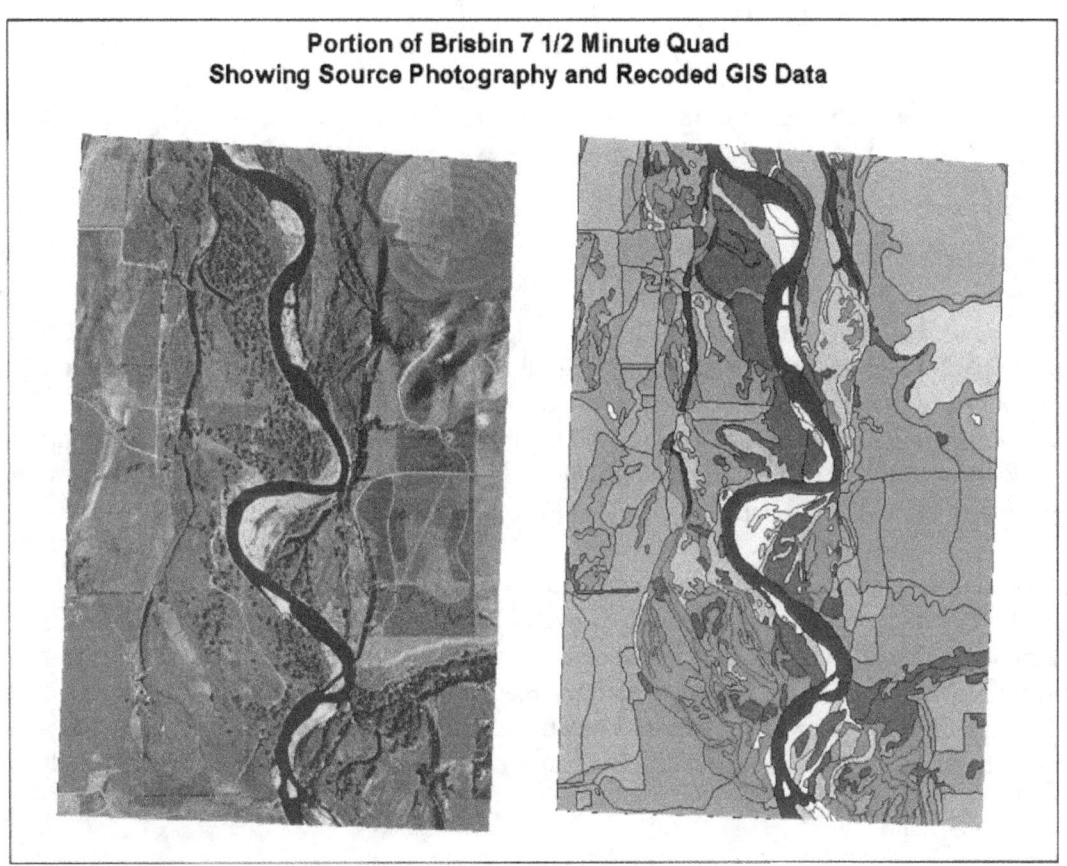

Portion of Brisbin 7 1/2 Minute Quad
Showing Source Photography and Recoded GIS Data

Photo Interpretation

Wetland, riparian and upland land use/land cover boundary delineation and classification was accomplished through stereoscopic interpretation of the aerial photography using established Service procedures and protocols found in "Photointerpretation Conventions for the National Wetlands Inventory" (USFWS 1995). Features large enough for a photo interpreter to delineate an entire boundary around were delineated as polygons so area measurements were as accurate as possible. Features too narrow to delineate as a polygon were delineated with a single dashed line or linear. A point is a feature so small that a single dot delineates it. Linear and point data are buffered during area calculations and included in the acreage figures in the text to make them as accurate as possible. Although linear and point data may seem minor in comparison to polygon data they are still a significant portion of the overall habitat in the Yellowstone River study area.

5

Stereoscopic color-infrared photographs are most suitable for identifying wetland and riparian habitats. Color, texture, pattern and physiographic position are important features of these habitats that can be identified best on this type of photography. Land use and land cover can be identified equally well. Wetland vegetation is generally more dense and exhibits a higher degree of lushness and vigor than does either upland or riparian vegetation. The vegetative factors that combine to produce a specific response or photographic signature include color, shape, growth habit, height, branching pattern and leaf size. When stereoscopically viewed physiographic positions are associated with these vegetative characteristics, wetland locations and boundaries become more obvious on an aerial photograph. Riparian habitats are identified in a similar manner but are generally higher in the physiographic profile and less dense and lush. Upland land use and land cover can be identified mainly by evidence of human habitation and modification.

Combining field work to correlate photo signatures to specific habitat types or land use with the above methods allows an experienced photo interpreter to extrapolate based on patterns to areas not checked in the field. Generally this produces a very accurate product. However, due to the fact that a photograph is simply a snapshot in time, variations can occur between the date of photography and the present time. Some errors of omission and commission may also occur as with any data produced using remotely sensed technologies. Natural Resources Conservation Service soil surveys and United States Geological Survey topographic maps and water resource data were primary collateral data sources used to increase the accuracy of the mapping.

Wetlands and deepwater habitats were classified according to "Classification of Wetlands and Deepwater Habitats of the United States" (Cowardin et al. 1979), the Department of the Interior standard for technical wetland identification and classification. Riparian habitats were classified according to "A System for Mapping Riparian Areas in the Western United States" (1997), the U.S. Fish and Wildlife Service standard. Land use and land cover was classified according to "A Land Use and Land Cover Classification System for Use with Remote Sensor Data" (Anderson et al. 1976).

Cartography
After the aerial photography was interpreted the delineations were transferred onto a 7 mil stable based sheet of mylar overlaying a black and white version of a 1:24,000 scale U. S. Geological Survey topographic base map using established Service procedures and protocols found in "Cartographic Conventions for the National Wetlands Inventory" (USFWS 1994). A special optical instrument called a Zoom Transfer Scope enabled a cartographic technician to view the delineated photograph superimposed on the topographic base map. The photograph delineations were then traced onto the overlain base map after which a 4 mil stable based mylar overlay was used for labeling. The three layers, USGS base map, linework overlay and lettering overlay, were then composited reprographically to complete map compilation and create final maps (Figure 3). The classifications are shown on the maps as alpha-numeric codes and are identified and explained in the legend at the bottom of the map.

Figure 3. Portion of an NWI map showing complexity of delineations.

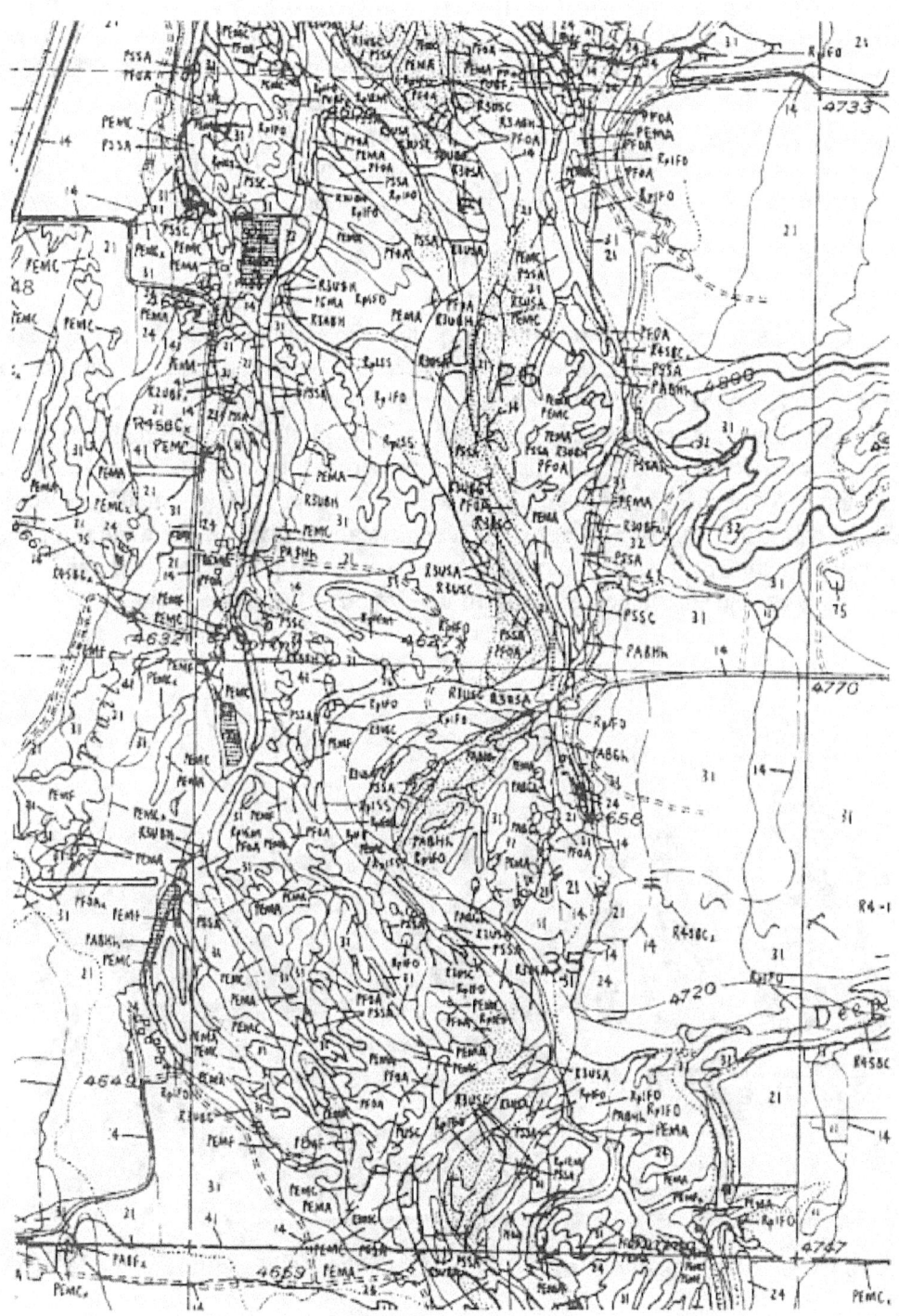

Digitization

The final map mylars were scanned digitally at a resolution up to 650 dpi (dots per inch) after which the pixel file was converted to recognizable lines and points by a raster to vector conversion program. WAMS (wetland analytical mapping software) was used interactively to assign wetland, riparian and upland attributes to each polygon, linear and point feature. WAMS also builds data topology and calculates polygon areas and linear feature lengths. This complete process creates a digital database in GIS form for computerized data analysis. This includes types and acreage statistics for all wetland, riparian and upland data and allows the production of ancillary products such as color-coded maps. Established Service procedures and protocols were followed as described in "Digitizing Conventions for the National Wetlands Inventory" (USFWS 1994).

Quality Control

Many quality control steps were performed throughout the mapping process from the original field work to correlate photo signatures to specific vegetative types and land use patterns to final quality control checks on the digital data. Photo interpretation delineations and classifications were checked. Draft maps were checked against the original photo delineations for accuracy in transfer of linework and labels. Digital data were processed through a series of verification programs including logic checks of wetland attributes for improper labels. In addition the resulting digital data consisting of attributes and acreage statistics was put through one final check for possible errors. Still, as with any remotely-sensed, computer generated data, there may exist errors although these should be insignificant in relation to the entire project.

Wetland (PFOA) and riparian (Rp1FO) forest along the Yellowstone River (R3UBH).

Mapping Conventions

Wetland

Wetlands were mapped according to "Classification of Wetlands and Deepwater Habitats of the United Stated" (Cowardin et al. 1979). In this system wetlands are defined as:

> ". . . lands transitional between terrestrial and aquatic systems where the water table is usually at or near the surface or the land is covered by shallow water. For the purposes of this classification wetlands must have one or more of the following three attributes: (1) at least periodically, the land supports predominantly hydrophytes [wetland plants], (2) the substrate is predominantly undrained hydric soil, and (3) the substrate is nonsoil [does not support vegetation] and is saturated with water or covered by shallow water at some time during the growing season of each year."

This classification system is hierarchical where habitats are classified according to system, subsystem and class. Water regime and special modifiers can also be added. Five systems are described in this classification, two of which occur along the Yellowstone River. These two systems are: riverine (rivers, streams and their associated sand and gravel bars) and palustrine (swamps, marshes, wet meadows, fens, bogs and small, shallow ponds).

Each separate wetland type is labeled with a corresponding code or alpha-numeric (Appendix A). As users proceed through any individual wetland classification more information is provided for that particular wetland. For example, the Yellowstone River is classified as R3UBH where:

R represents the riverine *system* defined as:
> "all wetlands and deepwater habitats contained within a channel with two exceptions: (1) wetlands dominated by trees, shrubs, persistent emergents, emergent mosses, or lichens, and (2) habitats with water containing ocean-derived salts in excess of 0.5%."

3 represents the upper perennial *subsystem* where:
> "The gradient is high and velocity of water is fast. There is no tidal influence and some water flows throughout the year. The substrate consists of rock, cobbles, or gravel with occasional patches of sand. The natural dissolved oxygen concentration is normally near saturation. The fauna is characteristic of running water, and there are few or no planktonic forms. The gradient is high compared with that of the Lower Perrenial Subsystem, and there is little floodplain development."

UB represents the unconsolidated bottom *class* defined as:

> "all wetland and deepwater habitats with at least 25% cover of particles smaller than stones, and a vegetative cover less than 30%. Unconsolidated Bottoms are characterized by the lack of large stable surfaces for plant and animal attachment."

H represents the permanently flooded *water regime* where:

> "Water covers the land surface throughout the year in all years. Vegetation is composed of obligate hydrophytes."

For a more detailed explanation of NWI map codes, consult the U.S. Fish and Wildlife Service's 1993 publication "NWI Maps Made Easy: A User's Guide to National Wetlands Inventory Maps of the Mountain-Prairie Region", or the USFWS 1999 publication "Mapping Conventions Used to Identify Wetlands Within the Northern Rocky Mountains and Great Plains".

Riparian

Riparian habitats were mapped according to the U. S. Fish and Wildlife Service standard, "A System for Mapping Riparian Areas in the Western United States" (1997). This system defines riparian as:

> ". . . plant communities contiguous to and affected by surface and subsurface hydrologic features of perennial or intermittent lotic [flowing] and lentic [still] water bodies (rivers, streams, lakes or drainage ways). Riparian areas have one or both of the following characteristics: 1) distinctly different vegetative species than adjacent areas, and 2) species similar to adjacent areas but exhibiting more vigorous or robust growth forms. Riparian areas are usually transitional between wetland and upland."

The riparian system is hierarchical and uses system, subsystem, and class as well as the optional subclass and dominance types (Appendix B). An example of a riparian habitat that was mapped as a part of the Yellowstone River project is Rp1FO where:

Rp is the *system* and stands for riparian which is transitional between wetland and upland plant communities.

1 is the *subsystem* which reflects the water source for the riparian area and represents lotic or flowing water.

FO is the *class* which describes the dominant non-hydrophytic life form of riparian vegetation, in this case forested. Forested (FO) is defined as: "woody vegetation usually greater than 6 m. in height."

Subclasses and dominance types were not used for this mapping effort.

Gravel bar (R3USA) and wetland forested (PFOA) along Yellowstone River (R3UBH).

Upland

Upland areas were mapped according to the U. S. Geological Survey publication "A Land Use and Land Cover Classification System for Use with Remote Sensor Data" (Anderson et al. 1976). This system is a numerical classification system with three levels of detail, the first two of which were used for the Yellowstone River mapping effort (Appendix C). For example cropland and pasture is classified as 21 where:

2 is the level one classification and represents agricultural land defined as:
"land used primarily for production of food and fiber."

1 is the level two classification and represents specifically cropland and pasture which includes:
"cropland harvested, including bush fruits; cultivated summer-fallow and idle cropland; land on which crop failure occurs; cropland in soil-improvement grasses and legumes; cropland used only for pasture in rotation with crops; and pasture on land more or less permanently used for that purpose."

Figure 4 shows examples and descriptions of wetland, riparian and upland terminology.

Figure 4. Examples of Classification Terminology

Wetland Code	Common Description and/or Examples
R3UBH	Main river channel, Yellowstone River. Water flows year round.
R3UBG/F	Smaller streams or channels that may dry up periodically
R3USA/C	Sand or gravel bars along a river
R4SBC/A	Intermittent streams that flow only part of every year
PABH/G/F	Pond with aquatic plants, many times either excavated or impounded (small x or h modifier)
PEMF/C/A	Emergent or herbaceous wetland plants
PSSC/A	Woody plants less than 6 meters in height. The majority of scrub-shrub along the river channels and in the floodplain were classified as seasonally flooded (C). The majority of scrub-shrub on the river bars were classified as temporarily flooded (A).
PFOC/A	Woody plants over 6 meters in height. The majority of wet trees were classified as temporarily flooded (A).

Riparian Code	
Rp1FO	Trees insufficiently inundated to satisfy the wetland criteria but which derive their vigor and robustness from an adjacent stream or river. The majority of riparian trees were below the third terrace of the Yellowstone River or along tributaries.
Rp1SS	Shrubs insufficiently inundated to satisfy the wetland criteria but which derive their vigor and robustness from an adjacent stream or river. The majority of riparian shrubs were along the Yellowstone River or tributaries.
Rp1EM	Herbaceous plants insufficiently inundated to satisfy the wetland criteria but which derive their vigor and robustness from an adjacent river or stream. Many areas of riparian emergent vegetation occur on hydric or fluvial soils as delineated on soil survey maps of the area. If the area was not wet enough for a wetland designation and did not appear to be upland it was delineated as riparian.

Upland Code	
11	Residential areas
14	Transportation (roads), communication (telephone facilities) and utilities (power substations)
21	Cropland and pasture
24	Other agricultural land such as farmsteads and corrals
31	Herbaceous rangeland
75	Barren land within strip mines, quarries and gravel pits

Products

A variety of products were produced for this project. In addition to this report, 1:24,000 scale hard copy final paper maps were prepared. These consist of the wetland, riparian and land use/land cover delineations overlayed on a copy of the USGS topographic map for each quadrangle (Figure 3). Final maps are available from the Regional Map Distribution Center in Brookings, South Dakota at 605-688-5890. Arc Info digital data consisting of a wetland, riparian and land use/land cover layer were produced from these maps for use in geographical information systems. Digital data can be downloaded through the NWI home page on the Internet at http://www.nwi.fws.gov. Polygon acreage, linear miles and point summaries for all wetland, riparian and upland features were also produced for each of the fourteen quads in the study area. A variety of ancillary products such as color-coded maps and plots may be produced using the digital data in conjunction with a GIS.

Results

Polygon features are measured during the digitization process to obtain areas in acres. Linear and point data are buffered during area calculations and included in the acreage figures in the text to make them as accurate as possible. Linear distances are listed in miles on the feature summaries and were converted to acreages on the assumption that they have an average width of 10 feet. Points are listed by frequency or number and were converted to acreages assuming each point averages 0.1 acre.

Although linear and point data may seem minor in comparison to polygon data they are still a significant portion of the overall data in the Yellowstone River study area. For example, there are 167 miles or 203 acres of roads that were mapped as linear features in the study area (Appendix F).

Riverine and Palustrine Wetlands
The National Wetlands Inventory identified and mapped 55 categories of wetlands and deepwater habitats occupying 7,750 acres in the Yellowstone River project area (Appendix D). These figures include buffered linear and point data. All wetlands identified were classified in two systems, riverine and palustrine. Riverine wetlands and deepwater habitats (including sand and gravel bars) make up the largest percentage of wetland habitats and cover 4,198 acres or 54 percent of all wetlands within the project area. Rivers and streams in this area are either intermittent with water flowing only a part of the year, or perennial where some water flows throughout the year. The majority of perennial rivers and streams in the project area are upper perennial with the Yellowstone River itself comprising the largest feature of this type. Ninety seven percent by area of streams in the project area are upper perennial. Unconsolidated

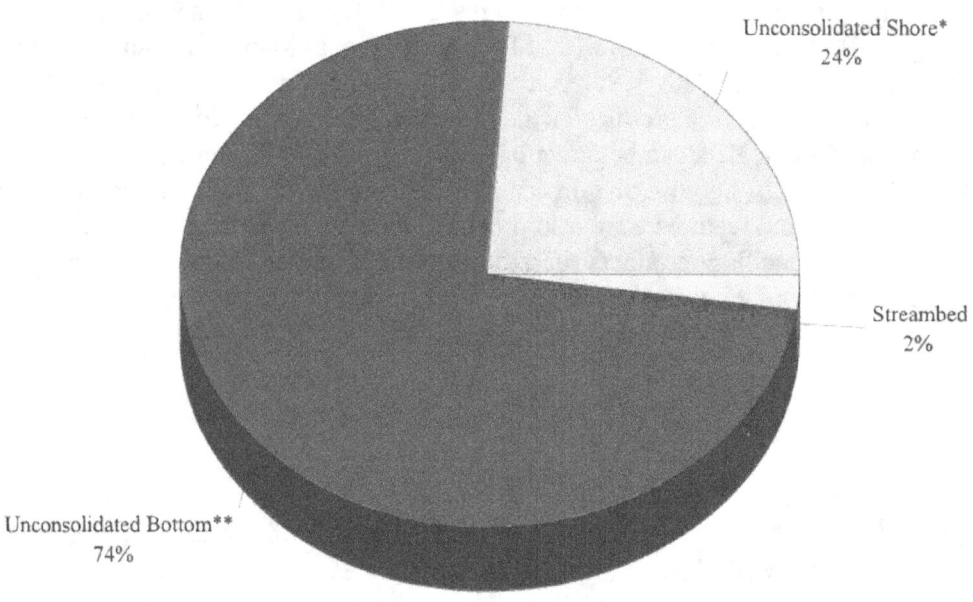

Unconsolidated Shore*
24%

Streambed
2%

Unconsolidated Bottom**
74%

Figure 5. Open water dominates the riverine system although there is a significant amount of sand and gravel bars. *Includes sand and gravel bars. **Includes open water and aquatic bed.

shore (gravel bars) makes up 24 percent of all riverine classes at 1,010 acres with unconsolidated bottom and aquatic bed (open water), which generally relates to the main channel, accounting for 74 percent or 3,122 acres. The streambed class, found only within the intermittent riverine sub-system, makes up the remaining 2 percent at 66 acres (Figure 5).

The remaining 46 percent or 3,552 acres of wetland habitat are palustrine wetlands, of which 1,675 acres (47 percent) are emergent or herbaceous, 1,042 acres (29 percent) are scrub/shrub and 664 acres (19 percent) are forested wetlands. The remaining 171 acres (5 percent) of palustrine wetlands are either non-vegetated (unconsolidated bottom or shore) or aquatic bed (Figure 6). Vegetated wetlands along streams and rivers are classified as palustrine even though the stream hydrology may have created them and sustains them. Most of the forested wetlands, a high percentage of the scrub/shrub wetlands and a significant portion of the emergent wetlands are related directly to river hydrology.

14

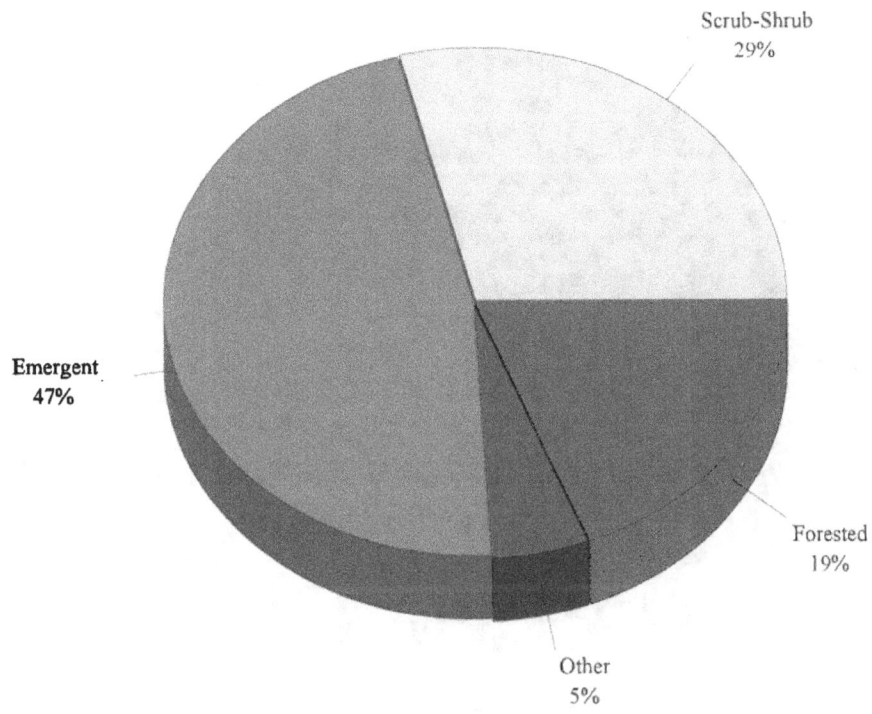

Figure 6. Vegetated wetlands are distributed throughout the palustrine system with the emergent class the most dominant. Small percentages of unconsolidated bottom, unconsolidated shore, and aquatic bed constitute the "Other" category.

Riparian Habitat

There were 18 categories of riparian habitat identified and mapped which total 3,078 acres within the project area (Appendix E). This includes buffered linear data and also mixed wetland/riparian habitats which were mapped together because of scale limitations (for example: R4SBA-Rp1Fo linear features). This example is an illustration of a narrow linear where the riparian forested is so inter-mixed with the riverine streambed that it is impossible to delineate them separately. Rather than delineate areas such as these as either wetland or riparian they were delineated as both to obtain as much information as possible.

Virtually all (greater than 99 percent) of the riparian habitat in the study area is lotic or related to flowing water, the vast majority attributable to the Yellowstone River. Riparian forested habitat comprises the largest riparian category at 2,621 acres or 85 percent of all riparian habitat. Riparian scrub/shrub habitat totaled 92 acres or 3 percent. Riparian emergent habitat (herbaceous communities) totaled 365 acres or 12 percent (Figure 7).

15

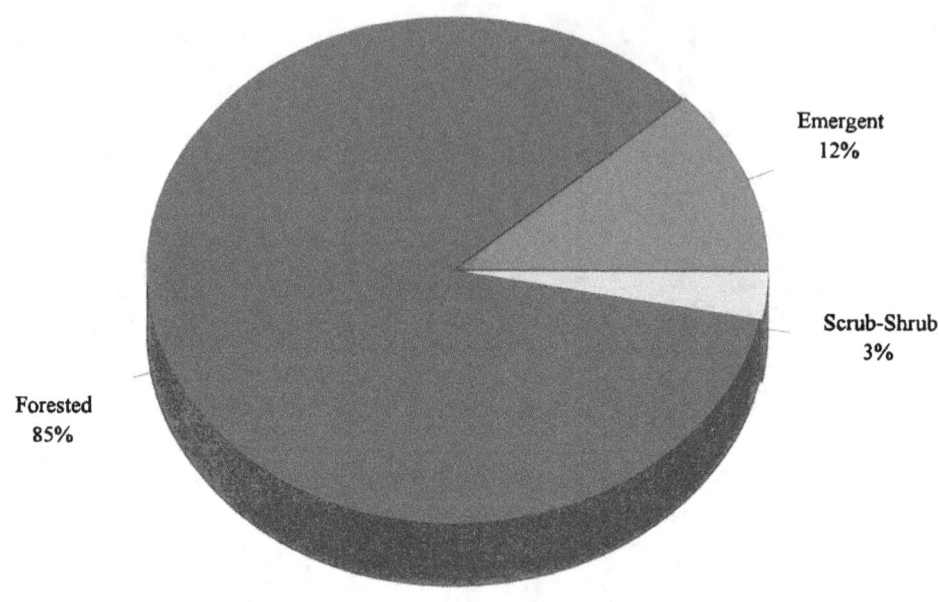

Emergent
12%

Scrub-Shrub
3%

Forested
85%

Figure 7. Forested habitat dominates the riparian system within the Yellowstone River study area.

Upland
Five level one and nineteen level two categories of upland land use and land cover totaling 43,932 acres were identified and mapped in the project area. This figure includes buffered linears such as roads but no point data (Appendix F). Rangeland comprises the largest level one category at 22,023 acres or 50 percent of all upland within the study area. Agricultural land is the second largest level one category at 15,537 acres or 35 percent. Urban or built-up land covers 5,494 acres or 13 percent of the study area. The remaining 2 percent, 878 acres, is divided between barren land (mostly gravel pits and rock outcrops), and forest land (Figure 8).

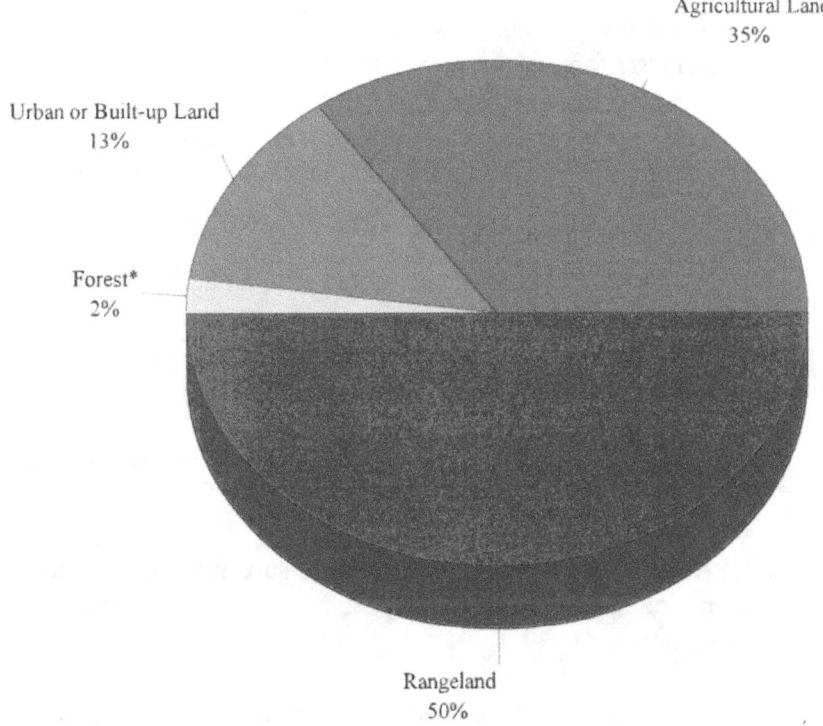

Agricultural Land
35%

Urban or Built-up Land
13%

Forest*
2%

Rangeland
50%

Figure 8. Rangeland dominates the upland land use/land cover within the project area with agricultural and urban land constituting most of the remainder.
*Includes a small percentage of barren land.

The largest percentage of rangeland is herbaceous rangeland (31) at 94 percent, the remaining 6 percent being shrub and brush rangeland. Ninety-three percent of agricultural land is the level two category of cropland and pasture (21). The majority of urban acreage is composed of transportation corridors (14) and towns such as Livingston (16 or mixed urban).

Definitions

Following are definitions of some technical terms as found in this document.

Digitize   The process of converting hard copy maps to digital or numeric form.

Dominant   The vegetative species or life form either controlling or most prevalent in the immediate environment. For this project, considered to be at least 30 percent vegetative cover.

Emergent   A species that is erect and rooted with an herbaceous stem.

Emulsion   The coating on photographic films which gives aerial photos their distinctive colors.

Growth Form   Generally related to vigorous health, compactness, crowding and/or numbers of individuals.

Hydrophyte   Any plant growing in water or on a substrate that is at least periodically deficient in oxygen as a result of excessive water content.

Mil   A unit of measure used in measuring the thickness of film.

Mylar   A form of polyester made in extremely thin sheets of great tensile strength. Used for drafting maps and photographic reproduction.

Pixel   An element of a photograph. The basic, smallest unit of which an image is composed.

Raster   A data format in which the data elements are represented as cells or pixels. Cells can be strung together to represent lines and polygons.

Remote Sensing   The acquisition or measurement of information by a recording device at a distance. For example, aerial photography.

Signature   Any characteristic or series of characteristics by which something may be recognized. For example, photographic signature.

Vector   A data format in which the data elements are represented as points, lines or polygons and are referenced to a spatial location.

Literature Cited

Anderson, J.R., E.E. Hardy, J.T. Roach, R.E. Witmer. 1976. A land use and land cover classification system for use with remote sensor data. U.S. Geological Survey, Washington, DC. Professional Paper 964.

Cowardin, L.M., V. Carter, F.C. Golet and E.T. LaRoe. 1979. Classification of wetlands and deepwater habitats of the United States. U.S. Fish and Wildlife Service, Washington, DC. FWS/OBS 79-31. 103 pp.

U.S. Fish and Wildlife Service. 1997. A system for mapping riparian areas in the western United States. Washington, D.C. 15 pp.

U.S. Fish and Wildlife Service. 1993. NWI Maps Made Easy: A User's Guide to National Wetlands Inventory Maps of the Mountain-Prairie Region. Denver, CO. 16 pp.

U.S. Fish and Wildlife Service. 1994a. Cartographic Conventions for the National Wetlands Inventory. U.S. Fish and Wildlife Service, St. Petersburg, FL. 71 pp.

U.S. Fish and Wildlife Service. 1994b. Digitizing Conventions for the National Wetlands Inventory. U.S. Fish and Wildlife Service, St. Petersburg, FL. 21 pp.

U.S. Fish and Wildlife Service. 1995. Photointerpretation Conventions for the National Wetlands Inventory. U.S. Fish and Wildlife Service, St. Petersburg, FL. 60 pp.

U. S. Fish and Wildlife Service. 1999. Mapping Conventions Used to Identify Wetlands Within the Northern Rocky Mountains and Great Plains: A Guide to Understanding National Wetlands Inventory Mapping Codes. U.S. Fish and Wildlife Service, Denver, CO. 31 pp.

All photographs were taken by Kevin W. Bon,
U. S. Fish and Wildlife Service and Jim Robinson,
Montana Department of Natural Resources.

Appendix A. National Wetlands Inventory Map Legend used for the Yellowstone River.

SYSTEM	SUBSYSTEM	CLASS

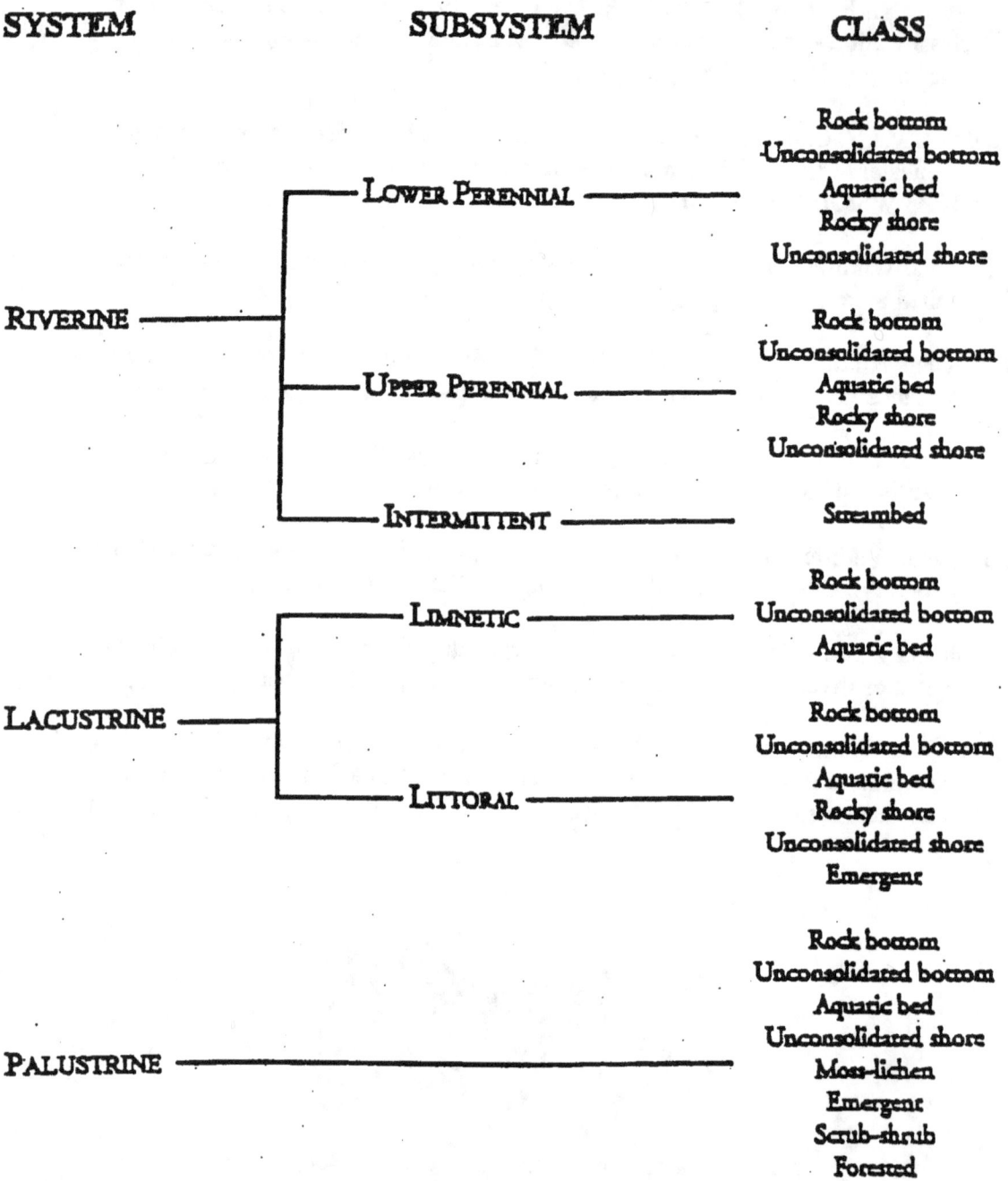

	LOWER PERENNIAL	Rock bottom Unconsolidated bottom Aquatic bed Rocky shore Unconsolidated shore
RIVERINE	UPPER PERENNIAL	Rock bottom Unconsolidated bottom Aquatic bed Rocky shore Unconsolidated shore
	INTERMITTENT	Streambed
LACUSTRINE	LIMNETIC	Rock bottom Unconsolidated bottom Aquatic bed
	LITTORAL	Rock bottom Unconsolidated bottom Aquatic bed Rocky shore Unconsolidated shore Emergent
PALUSTRINE		Rock bottom Unconsolidated bottom Aquatic bed Unconsolidated shore Moss-lichen Emergent Scrub-shrub Forested

WATER REGIMES		SPECIAL MODIFIERS
A. Temporarily flooded	G. Intermittently exposed	b. Beaver
B. Saturated	H. Permanently flooded	d. Partially drained
C. Seasonally flooded	J. Intermittently flooded	h. Diked/Impounded
F. Semipermanently flooded	K. Artificially flooded	x. Excavated

Appendix B. Riparian Habitat Map Legend used for the Yellowstone River.

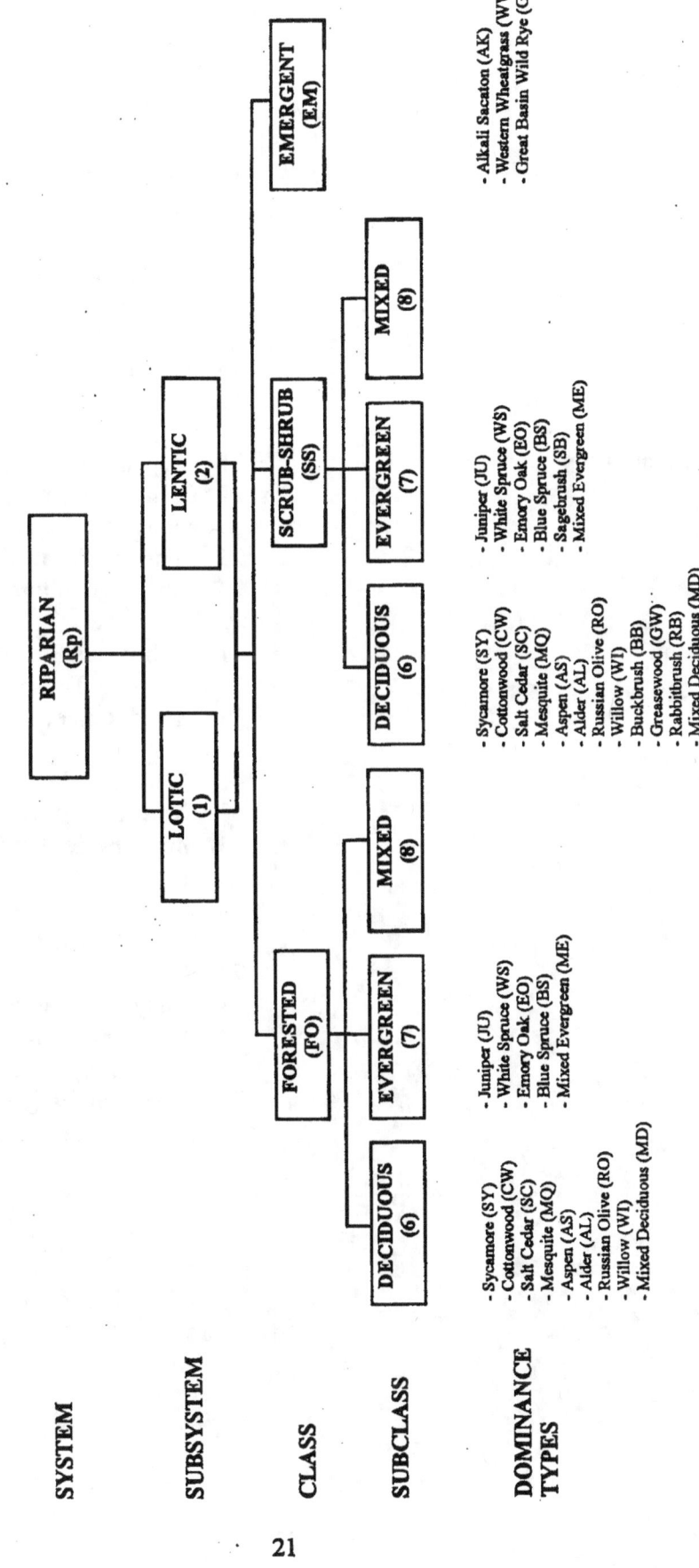

SYSTEM

SUBSYSTEM

CLASS

SUBCLASS

DOMINANCE
TYPES

RIPARIAN
(Rp)

LOTIC
(1)

LENTIC
(2)

FORESTED
(FO)

SCRUB-SHRUB
(SS)

EMERGENT
(EM)

DECIDUOUS
(6)

EVERGREEN
(7)

MIXED
(8)

DECIDUOUS
(6)

EVERGREEN
(7)

MIXED
(8)

- Sycamore (SY)
- Cottonwood (CW)
- Salt Cedar (SC)
- Mesquite (MQ)
- Aspen (AS)
- Alder (AL)
- Russian Olive (RO)
- Willow (WI)
- Mixed Deciduous (MD)

- Juniper (JU)
- White Spruce (WS)
- Emory Oak (EO)
- Blue Spruce (BS)
- Mixed Evergreen (ME)

- Sycamore (SY)
- Cottonwood (CW)
- Salt Cedar (SC)
- Mesquite (MQ)
- Aspen (AS)
- Alder (AL)
- Russian Olive (RO)
- Willow (WI)
- Buckbrush (BB)
- Greasewood (GW)
- Rabbitbrush (RB)
- Mixed Deciduous (MD)

- Juniper (JU)
- White Spruce (WS)
- Emory Oak (EO)
- Blue Spruce (BS)
- Sagebrush (SB)
- Mixed Evergreen (ME)

- Alkali Sacaton (AK)
- Western Wheatgrass (WW)
- Great Basin Wild Rye (GB)

Appendix C. Upland Land Use/Land Cover Classification Legend.

Level I	Level II
1 Urban or Built-up Land	11 Residential
	12 Commercial and Services
	13 Industrial
	14 Transportation, Communications and Utilities
	15 Industrial and Commercial Complexes
	16 Mixed Urban or Built-up Land
	17 Other Urban or Built-up Land
2 Agricultural Land	21 Cropland and Pasture
	22 Orchards, Groves, Vineyards, Nurseries and Horticultural Areas
	23 Confined Feeding Operations
	24 Other Agricultural Land
3 Rangeland	31 Herbaceous Rangeland
	32 Shrub and Brush Rangeland
	33 Mixed Rangeland
4 Forest Land	41 Deciduous Forest Land
	42 Evergreen Forest Land
	43 Mixed Forest Land
7 Barren Land	71 Dry Salt Flats
	72 Beaches
	73 Sandy Areas other than Beaches
	74 Bare Exposed Rock
	75 Strip Mines, Quarries and Gravel Pits
	76 Transitional Areas
	77 Mixed Barren Land

Appendix D-1. Wetland Polygon Acreage Summary.

Classification	Acres
PABF	16.607
PABFh	10.925
PABFx	7.417
PABG	15.063
PABGb	0.455
PABGh	5.926
PABGx	1.899
PABHh	32.383
PABKx	4.166
PEMA	920.109
PEMAd	16.166
PEMAh	0.190
PEMAx	1.778
PEMB	3.869
PEMC	470.019
PEMCd	6.242
PEMCh	0.814
PEMCx	2.395
PEMF	109.083
PEMFh	2.137
PEMFx	2.644
PFOA	632.420
PFOAx	2.913
PFOC	11.498
PSSA	783.967
PSSAx	1.463
PSSB	0.444
PSSC	216.845
PSSCx	1.547
PUBF	0.467
PUBFx	29.658
PUBGx	35.334
PUSC	0.804
PUSCx	5.609
R2UBFx	0.471
R2UBG	2.688
R2USA	12.983
R2USC	1.798
R3ABH	30.198
R3UBF	5.455
R3UBG	10.071
R3UBH	3,015.681
R3USA	839.709
R3USC	137.194
	7,409.504

Appendix D-2. Wetland Linear Miles Summary.

Classification	Miles
PABF	0.982
PABFh	0.804
PABFx	0.379
PABG	0.955
PABGh	0.158
PEMA	7.266
PEMAx	1.577
PEMC	13.655
PEMCx	76.310
PEMF	7.342
PEMFh	0.153
PEMFx	8.402
PFOA	8.331
PFOAh	0.092
PFOAx	5.215
PFOC	0.271
PSSA	24.207
PSSAh	0.057
PSSAx	0.650
PSSC	4.369
PSSCx	1.469
PUBFx	0.194
PUSCx	0.015
R2UBF	0.784
R2UBFx	19.604
R2UBG	2.373
R2UBHx	0.117
R2USA	0.027
R3ABH	0.194
R3UBF	6.668
R3UBFx	0.215
R3UBG	11.219
R3UBGx	0.119
R3UBH	5.968
R3USA	7.119
R3USC	7.913
R4SBA	2.791
R4SBAx	2.110
R4SBC	4.272
R4SBCx	45.332
	279.678

Appendix D-3. Wetland Point Summary.

Classification	Frequency
PEMA	3
PEMAx	1
PEMC	3
PEMFh	2
PUBFx	1
PUSCh	1
	11

Appendix E-1. Riparian Polygon Acreage Summary.

<u>Classification</u>	<u>Acres</u>
R4SBA-Rp1FO	0.140
Rp1EM	360.745
Rp1FO	2,599.968
Rp1SS	81.807
Rp2FO	1.370
Rp2SS	0.215
	3,044.245

Appendix E-2. Riparian Linear Miles Summary.

Classification	Miles
PEMA-Rp1FO	0.061
PEMAx-Rp1FO	0.221
PEMC-Rp1FO	0.242
PEMCx-Rp1FO	1.230
PEMCx-Rp1SS	0.167
R2-Rp1FO	0.687
R2-Rp1SS	1.239
R2UBF-Rp1FO	0.472
R4-Rp1FO	3.071
R4-Rp1SS	2.826
R4SBA-Rp1FO	0.334
R4SBCx-Rp1FO	0.521
R4SBCx-Rp1SS	0.341
Rp1EM	3.642
Rp1FO	8.961
Rp1SS	3.786
Rp2FO	0.350
	28.151

Appendix F-1. Upland Polygon Acreage Summary.

Classification	Acres
11	403.888
12	70.345
13	64.898
14	1,971.385
15	112.743
16	2,537.089
17	130.651
21	14,503.032
22	36.167
23	23.598
24	974.214
31	20,729.660
32	1,291.092
41	195.645
42	474.252
43	21.821
74	17.985
75	143.447
76	14.531
	43,716.443

Appendix F-2. Upland Linear Miles Summary.

Classification	Miles
14	167.377
32	1.547
41	0.503
42	8.280
	177.707

www.ingramcontent.com/pod-product-compliance
Lightning Source LLC
Chambersburg PA
CBHW080748290526
45790CB00008B/3377